IF I WERE MADE OF GLASS

Poetry Collection

Kelley Morris

Potter's Grove Press 2021

The following were first published on The Drabble:
Pieces - June 30, 2020
One More Time (as Grandma's Piano) – February 16, 2020
Lifted - -April 17, 2020
Reflections – August 4, 2018

Kelley Morris
www.pianogirlthoughts.com

First Printing: June 2021

Potter's Grove Press, LLC
www.pottersgrovepress.com

ISBN-13 - **978-1-951840-35-8**

To my Mom for sharing her love of poetry. And to my friend, Marina, for always reading my words back to me.

CONTENTS

IN THE BACKGROUND

What if the
Whole of me
Was on display
Not just one
Tiny window
Showing only
My face to all
Looking in, but
An entire house
Made of glass
Allowing light
Into every crevice
Of my being
Even in the quiet
Corners of my heart
Where only
A certain few
Are allowed to look
Would those
Who peer inside
Truly see me for me
Or only the things
I have carefully placed
In the background

MOTIVE

What is the motive
Behind my words
To cover a truth
Buried deep
Inside my core
Or reflect a
Desire for peace
To warm cold souls
Deceitful smiles
Worked tirelessly
To transform those
Once-searching into
Icy, untouchable stones
Now harboring hurt
Erasable only by
Kind sincerity
No motive for self
Indeed, a challenge
But one worth
Accepting
Words of affection
Spoken to thaw
The hardest of hearts

I'M LISTENING

Please come in,
I say to myself
Have a seat in your favorite chair.

Coffee?
Thank you. That would be nice.
We finally have time to catch up.

Yes, I know you prefer to listen.
But not today-It's your turn to talk.
My head is full of thoughts, you know.

Time to say them out loud. Nervous?
Well, yes. A little, I suppose.
But you are right. It is time.

Don't be afraid,
I say to myself.
Start talking, I'm listening.

LIKE A CHILD

To laugh and play
On the swings
Pumping feet
Back and forth
Flying high
Until a brave
Jump launches
Toward the sky

To show love
Skipping across
The playground
Hand in hand
With a friend
Spinning around
Falling down
On the ground

To speak truth
I love you
Immediately
Followed by
Your hair looks funny
Honest words
Unfiltered and
Straightforward

To seek security
In the comfort
Of a father's lap
Curled up in
Perfect rest
Breaths in sync
Every ounce of
Tension fading

To press rewind
Erasing today's
Apprehensions
Long enough to
See our world
Like a child-
Thru open eyes
Filled with wonder

SAFETY NET

Grandma and Grandpa
Lived next door
Aunts, Uncles, and
Cousins numbered
In double digits
Big kids played
With little kids
Running, laughing
Growing stronger
And bigger with
Each passing year
The knowledge
That no matter
How far I fell
Someone would
Catch me
Just like a
Little child
Bouncing on
A knee-
Ride a
Little horsey
Don't fall down-
A lasting security

Remaining strong
Despite passing time
And increasing distance
Living safety nets
Interwoven from one
Generation to the next

SMOOTH SURFACE

Rocks are fascinating
As a little girl, I loved
To collect them
Looking for unusual
Colors and shapes
Shiny veins running
Through the plain
A prized fossil
Sparking imagination-
What long-ago creature
Left their impression
Behind in stone?
Seemed like a magical feat-
Thinking about rocks now
I'm amazed by how
They grow more
Beautiful with the
Passing of time
And their surfaces
Become increasingly
Silky smooth with the
Weathering of storms

BLUE IRIS

I remember
The colors in
Our front yard
A row of
Beautiful blues
A row of
Bright yellows
The blues are
The ones I see
When my eyes
Are closed tight
And even though
They are far away
I can almost smell
Their sweet scent
...grape...
Childhood memories
Rows of blue iris
And my Mom
Standing in
The front yard

FRONT PORCH SWING

Legs crossed
One foot planted
Firmly on the floor
Securely guiding me
Back and forth
A gentle rocking
Not the flying
To the sky
Back and forth
Of childhood
No-this is
The swaying
Of contemplation
A vantage point
For the familiar-
Scenes now fuzzy
Thanks to frayed lines
On the well-worn
Window screens-
Yet, beauty remains
Holding power to
Release a rush of
Memories even
As clarity fades-

Renewed gratitude

Blurs restlessness with

Each motion felt

Each image seen

Each moment spent

On the front porch swing

BLUE-SKY EYES

Something about a
Bright blue sky
The color first
Catches my eye
Reminds me of
My Dad's eyes
Bright and true
Even a cloud
Drifting by
Cannot eclipse
Their honesty
Instead, the cloud
Brings clarity
Simply by contrast
Looking up
Toward the sky
I breathe in
The fresh air
It fills my lungs
Clears my head
Looking up
At my Dad
I feel safe
And loved
Thanks to the
Light in his
Blue-sky eyes

LIMITED SUPPLY

When young
Time seemed
An endless
Supply with
Little thought
Given to limits
Wished away in
A rush to meet
Each milestone
Without fully
Understanding
Its significance
Until years later
When the reality
Of limits became
Exceedingly clear
Times when
Life and death
Suddenly carried
Similar weight
Each new loss
A connection
To the past
Each new life
A hope for
The future
Quiet lessons
In limited supply

FOURTH OF JULY

He worked hard

His entire life

Married young

Raised nine kids

In the country

Strong and stubborn

Loved to laugh

Mellowed over time-

Without a doubt

Dealt with struggles

That I never knew

I see him in overalls

After a long day-

Promising to dance

At my wedding-

Liked to argue

Loved his family

Was always ready to

Welcome them home-

Looking forward to

Family gathering later

That very day-

But in the morning

While everyone slept

After waking early

Making the coffee

He sat in his favorite chair

At the young age of 67

Grandpa died on

The Fourth of July

SPILLED OUT

Some days
On the inside
I am still a child
Finding her way in this
Ever-changing world
Asking the same
Old questions-
Who am I?
Where do I belong?
What is my purpose?
What happens next?

Other days
On the outside
Wonder abounds
Light-lined clouds
Rumbling rolls of thunder
The rhythm of the rain
Offering answers-
Wife, mother, daughter
Right where you are
Exactly what you are doing
One day at a time

Confident answers
That blanket the
Cares of adulthood
In warm affection
Leaving behind
Newfound freedom
And transformation
Clouds become smiles
Thunder-outstretched hands
Rain-an arm around a shoulder
Gentle breeze-a baby's cry

I suppose that child
Will always be there
Some days filled
With questions
Other days listening
For answers that
Continually fill the
Heart with only
One purpose-
To be spilled right
Back out again

IN THE QUIET

The house is quiet

Guests have all

Gone home

Exhaustion

Resulting from a

Weekend long celebration

A momentous occasion

Symbolized by

Prayer and scripture

Rings and vows

Flowers and music

Beautiful bride

Handsome groom

Surrounded by friends

And family, making

A commitment to be

Faithful and true

In all things

Accepting each other's

Strengths and weaknesses

As they join their

Lives together

The wedding

A clear reflection

Of their hearts

A beautiful beginning

Faith, hope, and love

A lasting reassurance

Forever present

In the quiet

SAFE PASSAGE

The journey was
Not always what I
Thought it would be-
Rocking chairs
And lullabies
Bike rides and
Skinned knees
Tiny pieces of
A bigger picture
An incomplete map
Unfolding one
Step at a time-
The middle leg
Of the journey
Was much harder
A trusty compass
Guided through
Growing pains
Broken hearts
Moving, marriage
Letting go while
Pushing forward-
Current rest stop
Mixes deep joy

With sadness
Yet, comfort is
Found in knowing
These sweet souls
Entrusted to me
Received safe passage
Along this path of
Discovering what it
Means to be a mom

A GIFT

Mom wrote poems
Always with purpose
Remembering childhood
Honoring loved ones
Precious gifts
Bearing a message-
You hold importance
In my life-
Many live today
Displayed in the homes
Of friends and family
She wrote one for
My eleventh birthday
I can still see the
Holly Hobby paper
Sweet words written
In a neat cursive-
I love you
Where has the time gone?
Messages I did not
Understand until
Becoming a mom
Now, I write poems
Thankful for the gift-
Her thoughts on paper

BEAUTIFUL ECHO

So much learned by
Imitation, repetition
A baby's first words
Spoken over and over
The back and forth
Beautiful echo
Between parent and child
I remember my babies
Sitting in highchairs
Holding plastic shapes
Circle, square, triangle
I would trace them onto paper
Then gently hold their hands
As we retraced together
Repeating, smiling, celebrating
There are no more
New shapes to trace
New words to repeat
Now, I silently trace
Their hearts, their reactions
As they become my teachers-
Maybe they were
My teachers all along

WORTH REPEATING

I am not sure
I have ever
Considered myself strong
Oh, I can easily
Recall the times
I felt broken
Why is that?
Memories of weakness
Always surface first
Days that seemed eternal
Being dragged thru the dirt
Barely able to breathe-
Desperate for a cool
Drink of water-
I supposed those
Are the times that
Made me who I am
Made me strong-
There, I said it!
It is worth repeating!
I am strong!

BEHIND OUR EYES

What will I see
When I look
In your eyes
How many
Mysteries wait
Wanting to be
Discovered
Yet, your gaze
Remains downcast
I understand
Letting someone
Look into your eyes
Means looking
Into theirs-
Revealing what
Is hidden
On the inside-
It will be ok
Let's search for
A bit of trust
And just maybe
We will both
Be discovered
Accepting what waits
Behind our eyes

REMADE

An image shattered
Countless pieces
Strewn on the ground
A frightening scene
Of loss on display-
Those once interested
In pausing to look
Now quickly
Turn away
Murmuring-
Was the image even real?
An accurate representation?
Did it exist beyond the smile?
Answers don't matter-
For the one who
Remains close
Carefully picking
Up the pieces
Gently placing them
Back together
Knows the image
Remade with love
Will offer honesty

EXPLOSIONS

Many years between
Many words spoken
Too many to count
Yet, an equal number
Remained silent
You know the ones
Heat of the moment
Words so urgent
They'd surely explode
Inside my head
Unless spewed out
Into the open air-
Looking back
Remembering times
I chose to listen
Hearing what I
Most needed to hear
Words of love
Talking, laughing
And listening
Conversations that
Protected hearts
Keeping explosions
To a minimum

WARM BLANKET

Cold outside

Sun is shining

Sky is blue

But the air...brrr

Perfect paradox

When the visual

And physical

Do not match

Cold chills

My bones

As sunlight

Warms my face

One unable to

Fully exist

Without

The other

If my skin

Never felt

A chill, there'd

Be no joy in

A warm blanket

If my heart

Never knew

An icy touch

It would not

Know the warmth

Of your affection

Able to melt the

Coldest memories

REARVIEW

Cobwebs often
Remain hidden
Spinning webs
Unnoticed
Until thoughts
Begin to slow
And memories
Begin to fade
Collecting dust
Keeping love
From flowing
As it once did
A thorough sweeping
With a good broom
May be necessary
To clear away
The snares-or
Perhaps, a drive
Down memory lane
Taking us back
To the beginning
Where sparks fly
Memories flood
Love flows
Clearing out
The cobwebs
Leaving a dust trail
In the rearview

TRANSPARENT

Imagine a body
Translucent
Innocent as the skin
Of a newborn baby
No place to hide
Unprotected
Imagine eyes
Opened wide
Seeing everything
For the first time
With wonder
And uncertainty
Imagine a heart
Laid bare-open
For all to see
Joy and pain
On display
Simultaneously
Imagine these words-
I survived, so will you-
As we see each other
In transparent trust

OUT OF REACH

Some days the
Weight of worry
Presses down, heavy
And I am left crawling
Among the shadows
Hands and knees
Scraping the ground
Head low, feeling
Afraid and alone
Standing up
On my own
Is impossible-Yet,
A flicker of hope
Reminds me that
I *am not alone*
Like a child reaching
For their parent
I glance up as
His hands reach down
Lifting me out
Of the shadows
Gently placing me
Among the light
Of the stars

A time to rest
Preparation for
The day when
I will once again
Be found crawling
Among the shadows-
This is the journey-
To be traveled with
One lasting truth-
Wherever the road leads
I will *never* be
Out of reach

BELONGING

Hard to know
Where the sky
Ends and the
Earth begins
Snow-topped
Mountains blend
Into purple
And blue skies
Misty clouds
Gently blur
Greens in
Treetops
Calm ocean
Waters accept
Sunset reflections
Of pinks and reds
Perhaps there
Is no need to
See beginning
Or ending
Only a need
To recognize
Simple lessons
In belonging

CONFIDENCE BLOOMS

Tiny buds of worry
Anxiously wait
To be watered
Desiring to open
But hesitant
Unsure of responses
Will reactions
Be refreshing
Like a gentle rain,
Or harsh,
A downpour filled
With ice pellets?
One response holds
The power to make
The buds shrink
Overcome by
Uncertainty until
They wither and die
The other holds the
Promise of encouraging
The worry away
Gently watering
Watching and listening
As confidence blooms

FRESH AIR

Clouds cover the day
Like a heavy blanket
Intended to comfort
Instead, suffocating
Tossed over me
Without permission to
Hide what is good
Steal what is lovely-
Just as the wind
Chases away the clouds
My feet must
Kick off the cover
Wrestling that blanket
Until once again
The good is visible
The lovely restored-
My feet able to walk
Under the blue sky
Accepting the clouds
As a gentle umbrella
Offering protection
A sweet shelter
Allowing my heart to
Heal in the fresh air

HOLDING ON

Flashes of lightning
Crashing thunder
And howling winds
Disrupted any
Possibility for sleep
Morning remained dark
As the rain poured
Down from clouds-
Sunshine began to
Light the day
While silent
Remnants of
The evening storm
Hid in the breeze -
Hummingbirds flitted
Stopping briefly for
Sips of nectar-
One perched in
A nearby tree
Its tiny feet gripped
A skinny branch
As the leaf-covered
Limbs swayed
Back and forth-

This little miracle
Held firm and steady
While my tired heart
Watched in wonder
Listening to its message–
When the winds
Are tossing you
Back and forth
Just remember–
Keep holding on

TRUST

Morning birds
Sing their songs
Outside the window-
A quick look
Proves disappointing

Despite full feeders
There are no feathered
Friends in sight-
Singing continues
Hidden from view

Perhaps, it's a
Matter of trust
After too many
Days of visiting
Empty feeders?

They stopped coming-
The consistency and
Routine required to
Maintain any sense
Of trust was broken

Nourishment once
Freely provided was
No longer available-
Only for a short time
Yet, with consequences

Hiding replaced sharing
Security turned to fear-
Forgiveness takes time
Faith renewed only as
Needs are met once again

Feeders kept full
Under the shade
Of the trees
Day after day-
Regaining trust

A poignant truth
Regarding birds-
Yet, how much more
Important when
Speaking of people?

SILENT RIVER

Standing on its bank

All seems quiet

Water slowly

Drifts by

The movement

Difficult to perceive

Be still

Listen closely

Only then

Will the river

Share its stories

Of past travels

Around winding turns

Along cool stretches

Over rough rapids

Crashing on sharp rocks

Chasing the path ahead

Until finally, a free fall

Plunging to a clear pool below

A place of rest, where even

When still and silent

The river is telling its story

ABOVE AND BELOW

As I watch
The birds fly by
They seem to move
With such ease
Wings effortlessly
Gliding across
The wide blue

I imagine myself
Arms stretched out
From my sides
Winds carrying me
From place to place
My only responsibility-
Taking in the views

Except, there is
Effort required
Energy expelled
By flapping wings
Without which
The birds would
Fall from the sky

Why should it
Differ for me?
Why should I
Fly high above
The worries of
The day without
Giving my energy?

When given freely-
Every last drop,
If necessary-only
Then will I reap
Rewards of the
Beautiful views
Above and below

PRECIOUS CARGO

Small sticks and twigs
Soft pieces of lint
Maybe a leaf or two
Not a particularly strong
Sounding description for
A safe dwelling

Yet, the tiniest of birds,
Gather building materials
Carefully lacing
Each item with the next-
Until a soft bed is ready
To hold precious cargo

A little like the heart
Don't you think?
Small in comparison
To its host
Precisely as the nest
Is to the tree

Likewise held together
With strands of love
Gently knitted strong
Yet, soft enough
To hold close
Those I love

TAKE A SEAT

Walking alongside
The riverbank
Wondering what
It has to say
Tiny bits of
Wisdom heard
Only when
The water is
Still and quiet
Trees lean in
Close enough to
Notice changes
In the current-
These wise
Residents
Hold hands
Keeping the
Waterway
In place-
Sometimes
The bank is
Overtaken
When the river
Loses its way

It patiently waits
For the waters
To recede and
Continue on
Their journey
Strength
Evidenced in
Roots and trees
Dirt and rocks
Always faithful
Willing to give up
Part of itself
Every time
The river strays-
Wondering if
The riverbank
Will share some
Of its wisdom
While I quietly
Take a seat

BELOW THE SURFACE

Closely watching
The waters-
Yesterday, still as glass-
Smooth, giving no
Indication of motion
Underneath the surface-
Today, flashes of white
Warned of choppy seas
As winds from
Four directions
Met in the middle
Fighting over which way
The waves should flow-
Wisdom quietly shouted,
Stand back! Be still...
Strife always swirls
Below the surface
Curiosity asked,
What will tomorrow bring?
Wisdom replied,
That will depend
On your response...

LEGACY

The sun is setting
Out of sight
Out of mind
A cool breeze
Touches my face
As a stroll down
An empty sidewalk
Eases tensions
Allowing a few
Moments of peace
Turning the corner
A stifling reminder
The air no longer cool
Power left behind
By a forgotten sun
Western facing
Redbrick walls
Radiating heat
Received earlier
In the day
Stored for later use
A lasting legacy-
Remarkable strength
Revealed in
What is left behind

FROM MY WINDOW

Yesterday, the sun
Was brightly shining
Yet, offered no
Guarantee for today
I soaked in its rays
Warmed my face
Stared into the blue
Today, the storm came
Cooling the warmth
Of the sun
Erasing the blue
Of the sky
Traveling past
In a fury
I watched safely
From my window
Marveling at
Its strength
While wishing it
On its way
Hoping tomorrow
To once again
See light
Feel warmth
Stare deep

BEAUTIFUL ILLUSION

Time keeps ticking
Moving forward
Always steady
Always sixty
Seconds per minute
Minutes per hour
Never slows down
Never rushes ahead
If only I could
Stretch the moments
When my focus is clear
When my heart is full
Impossible, I know
Yet, I am able
To breathe deep
Allowing time for
A lingering hug
A heart-to-heart
Creating this
Beautiful illusion
Where time
Seems to stop
Mysteriously moving
Beyond the
Steady tick tock
Of the clock

ONE MORE TIME

The image remains

Though faded

Old and upright

Tall, black, majestic

Eighty-eight keys in a row

Sitting on the bench

Beautiful patterns

Come into focus

Two-three-two-three

A perfect guide

For little hands

Learning to play

Roll knuckles up

Tap twice

Repeat

Roll knuckles down

Tap twice

Repeat

I dropped

My dolly

In the dirt

A love that began

With simple melodies

Played on ivories

Prominently placed

In Grandma's

Dining room

How I wish

I could play

Those simple melodies

One more time

For my Grandma

On her old piano

BREATHING LIFE

I hear it first
In my memory
Although words escape
The tune is clear
One note leading
To the next
And the next
And on and on
A flawless sequence of sounds
Floating thru the air
Seamless as a priceless
String of pearls
Made perfectly complete
When notes in my head
Begin to journey
Thru my thoughts,
My eyes, my ears
Traveling the path to
My tired, aching fingers
Breathing life back
Into tired, weary bones

LINGERING

Impossible to count
The many notes
Played in places
Near and far
On pianos, grand
And ordinary
Yet, in certain
Circumstances
Melodies hang
In the air of
My memories
As if sounding
For the first time...
I remember sitting
At a familiar piano
My hands playing
Precious hymns
Honoring the life
Of my Grandma-
The music of both
Joy and sorrow
Where each note
Carries its own tear
Easing grief
While lingering
In the heart

GRIT

Tiny pieces of
Dust and rock
Able to slip
Into crevices
At first
Unnoticed
Creating only
Minor irritations
Until joined by
Other long-lost
Grating friends
Joining forces
Causing cracks
Disrupting even
The strongest
Of foundations

Displays of
Courage and
Determination
Within a vessel
Able to pour out
Inspiration into
Deep fractures

Distinguishable
From fakes
And forgeries
Lifting the worried
And anxious out
Of apprehension
Freely sharing to
Build up even the
Weakest foundations

Responses
To the first-
More irritating
Kind of grit-
Influences
One's ability to
Develop and
Freely share
The second-
More encouraging
Kind of grit-
Builds up
Instead of
Tearing down
Leaving behind
Deep reassurance

GRAVITY

The pressure
Begins to build
In the center
Of the chest
Pushing past
The heart
Welling up
In the throat
Seeking an
Escape route-
Tears falling
From my eyes
No consequence
Weight remains
Reason requires
Assistance
A temporary
Reprieve
Help from the
Unexpected
A song playing
On the radio
Laughing, I
Shake my head
Momentary release
From the gravity

GRACE

Not considering
Personal gain
Instead, seeing
Another in the
Light of grace
The same grace
Through which
Each one of
Us desires
To be seen
Grace that places
Selfish interest
Out of sight
Out of mind
Where it belongs
Two people
Face to face
One saying
I see you
I hear you
I want to know you
Not a request
An offering
Of friendship

SACRED SPACE

Sacred space
Sunrise to sunset
Precious hours
Waiting to be filled
Pleads with us
Accept the love
That wraps us up
In great affection
Eclipsing both
Light of day and
Dark of night
Avoid judgments
Leading to a critical spirit
Bitterness that bleeds
Into treasured time
Set aside for rest
Sacred space
Sunrise to sunset
Precious hours
Waiting to be filled

STOPPING TIME

What if I lie
Perfectly still
In the dark
Breaths shallow
Muscles relaxed
Surely time will
Stop for a moment
Allowing me a
Space to hold
One single note
Ringing in the air
A reminder of
Joy that sings
Even when
Days are hard
A simple request
One moment
Frozen in time
Melting away only
As your hand reaches
Through the darkness
To take hold of mine

UNBREAKABLE

Peace and love
Words that fit
Together seamlessly
But sorrow
And happiness
Don't belong in
The same line
Each word needs
Its own place
Fills its own space
Well, that's how
It would be
In a perfect world
But this world
Is not perfect
Honest reflection asks-
Should perfection
Be my goal, anyway?
Without deep sorrow
Can there be true happiness?
No simple answer
Only a mystery
One I must accept
Allowing its truth to

Sink way down deep
Into my soul, where
Sorrow and happiness
Are stitched together
An unbreakable seam
Holding the fabric of
My heart in place

SPOONFUL OF HONEY

Buzzing bee flits
From flower to flower
Briefly alighting on a petal
But not to rest
To scope out tiny
Grains of pollen
Gather them up
And fly back to its nest
Not its own singular nest
Like the one belonging to
The bluebird and her babies
No, a communal nest of
Endless golden hexagons
Joined together
To hold the future
Producing sweet
Healing goodness-
Suddenly the spoonful
Of honey that sweetened
My cup of tea this morning
Does not seem so simple

IMAGINE THAT

Fluffy white bear
Lying on its back
Feet up in the air
Happily playing
Oh, wait! Is that
A baby bear
It is bouncing
Up and down?
Like a dad
With his child
Smiling, laughing
Not a care in the world
Only one precious
Moment that can
Never be relived
That is how it goes
With pictures seen
In the clouds
If only the image
Could be recorded
A snapshot of the moment
Preserved for all to see
But that would
Defeat the purpose
Of Imagination
Where images last
Only as long as
Imagination and
The wind allows

CARRIED AWAY

Raindrops teased
All morning long
Falling a few at a time
With quiet drip-drops
Barely enough
To dampen the air
By late afternoon
The sky grew dark
No longer playing
Their little game,
The frightened raindrops
Huddled together
Creating steady streams
Flowing down from
Cloud to ground
Proving there is
Strength in numbers,
The brave raindrops
Transformed into
A wall of water
Like a transparent curtain
Hanging from the sky-
Suddenly, the curtain fell
No longer flowing

From cloud to sky

Now a blanket of water

Flowing downward

Across the landscape

Carrying away

All the sorrows

Of the day-

Then the sun began to shine

HOLE IN THE SKY

I saw a hole in
The sky today
Not deep or dark
Like a black hole
One might see
In outer space
No, a bright
Aperture
Glaringly
Reflective
Like light
Shining
On water
Curious what I
Might have seen
Had I been able to
Get a little closer
Wonder if
Anyone else
Noticed-or if
Maybe it was
Placed there
Just for me
A looking glass
Sharing a glimpse
Of the reality on
The other side of
The afternoon grays

WASTED TIME

Shh-be quiet
Listen closely to
The falling rain
Some might say
It is wasted time
Maybe the rain has
A story to tell
A fantastic tale
Of drops filling
Gray clouds
Until no matter how
Hard they try,
Can no longer
Hold the weight
The clouds give up
And the raindrops
Begin their freefall
At first, racing
To the ground
Finally landing
In perfect rhythm
Life-giving music
Serenading as it
Waters the earth

Providing a drink

For the flower

Sending relief

For the dry ground

Shh-be quiet

Listen closely to

The falling rain

It is not wasted time

By the time

You can hear it

The story is just beginning

SIGNIFICANT

The days seem long
Yet, they are not
When viewing them
Thru a wider lens

Getting caught up
In what's next
On the calendar
Is the expected

At least, that was
The case until
Our days were so
Abruptly changed

Life events often
Taken for granted
Now indefinitely
Placed on hold

And so, the small
Takes precedent
Kind words
An honest smile

A viewpoint
Revealing perhaps
The truly significant
Is actually quite small

HEAR OURSELVES

If only we could
Hear ourselves
Before words
Flow out into
The atmosphere
Letting them
Hang in the air-
Waiting until
The vowels
And consonants
Exclamation points
And question marks
Return to the
Mouth that spoke
Them into existence-
Would we choose
To suck them back
Into the lungs
Through the heart
Filtering out any
Selfish words
Removing any
Hateful words
Transforming them into
Messages of hope instead-
Surely our conversations
Would be different
If only we could
Hear ourselves

SEEING ME

Ever-present

All-around

Drifting in and

Out of sight

Head down

Hands in pockets

Woman standing

On the corner

Little boy sitting

On the playground

Lonely, forgotten

Left out of life

Simply existing

Outside of time

There is a choice

To be made

Keep moving

And ignore? Or

Stop and stand

In one place

Long enough

To see them

Long enough

To be seen

Long enough
To remember-
Only existing is
Not really living-
The next step?
Offer a smile
Walk toward them
Seeing me in them
Until they are
No longer left out

STANDING NEARBY

So many discussions
Even disagreements
Over the meaning
Of one simple word…
Neighbor
An age-old question-
Who is my neighbor?
One who lives next door
Across the street
A mile down the road
Descriptions that only begin
To scratch the surface-
Is it possible to be
Neighbors with no
Respect to distance?
In today's world-yes!
The next city
Another state
Across the world
But what about
The stranger who
Waits near me in a line
Walks into my classroom
Stands on the corner

One description does not
Negate the other
Does not lessen
My responsibility
To recognize a need
Find a way to give
Offer some kindness
Wherever I am standing
To whoever happens
To be standing nearby

PIECES

Broken bodies
Broken glass
Broken hearts

So many pieces to pick up
Although they may not be my own
They clearly lay in front of me
Scattered across the landscape

Of my city
Of my state
Of my country

Yet, love has not disappeared
It continues to weave
In and out of even the darkest days
Mingling with the broken pieces

Mending hearts
Mending lives
Mending souls

Offering flickers of hope
Amid feelings of despair
Showing us how to begin
Picking up the pieces

MASKS

One mask
Worn in
An attempt to
Hide insecurities
Creating a
Covering over
Anxious emotions
Though not physical
A protective shield
When worn
Only for
A short time
Another mask
Worn in
An attempt to
Fight sickness
Creating a
Material barrier
Between one person
And the next
Necessary
Yet, separating
Separating
Yet, protecting

Each mask

Tangible or ethereal

Serves to preserve

A way of life

An inward plea

Guard your heart

An outward plea

Protect your health

Lifesaving

Petitions that

Must never

Be ignored

Both masks

Providing an

Opportunity to see

Others in a new light

Both masks

Reminding us to

See beyond ourselves

CLOSE ENOUGH

I have never been one
For physical distance
Whether six feet or
Six-hundred miles
My preference
Will always be
Sitting next to you
Feeling your emotions
With each breath taken
Hearing your state of mind
In each word spoken
Letting your tears
Dampen my shoulder
My tears, yours
That is the space I prefer-
Close enough to laugh
Close enough to rest
Close enough to trust
Close enough to touch

HE HAS A NAME

Sad, empty face
Eyes distrusting
And suspicious
Tired-lonely
Beaten down
Shoulders slumped
No home-no
Place to rest
How? Why?
What series of
Events lead him
To this place?
Someone's dad?
Maybe
Someone's son?
An undeniable fact
He likes BBQ
Sandwiches and
Monster drinks-
That is all I know
Except that
Just like me
He is a person
Just like me
He has a soul
Inside that shell
Just like me
He has a name-
His name is Sam

MADE OF GLASS

If I were made of glass,
What shape would I take?
A vase for holding flowers
A bowl for sharing soup
A mug for embracing coffee
What shape would I want to take?
One that is useful, or
One intended only for display-
The thought of sitting on a shelf
Having contact with
The few who happen
To walk by and
Briefly gaze
Has little appeal
Although, it is
The one-place flaws
Are easily hidden
If hiding them
Serves any purpose-
After some thought
I think I'd prefer to
Live in the daylight
Allowing imperfections
To become reflective
Beauty in usefulness

DESTINATION

Denial is not
A particularly
Great state
To visit
And yet,
The plane
Has landed
Travel plans
Included much
More desirable
Destinations-
Nevertheless, here I am
Disembarking
Taking the ramp
Toward an unknown
Assistance required...
Needed...wanted...
Unsure which
Way to turn,
I keep looking
For the one
Holding a sign
With my name
Believing he will
Soon appear-
A guide thru
The unfamiliar-
Helping me reach
The intended destination

LIFTED

Lost track of time
Wandering in the
Shadows between
Light and dark

This will pass
I told myself
A feeble attempt
At reassurance

Then I hear…
Thinking of you
Are you ok?
Praying for you

Rays of sunshine
Breaking through
The haze to
Light my path

Cautiously I
Inched forward
Each step
Growing lighter

My spirit
Began to rise
As the fog
Lifted

A PEBBLE

Perhaps I have walked
Down the same road
Too many times
Sweet recollections
Influential lessons
Yet, wasted if
Only taken in
And not shared
Increasing danger
Of getting lost
In a circle of
Morals and memories
With little hope for
Real change in me
Or the world around
Instead, what if I
Remember this
Simple truth-
One pebble has the power
To create enormous waves-
And see my reflection
As a pebble tossed
Out into the water
Instantly changed
While creating change

NOT ALONE

Struggled to get
Out of bed
I would rather
Not admit
But if I'm
Being honest
Some days
I feel low
I move slowly
And the simple
Becomes difficult
Tears gather
Behind my eyes
Waiting for the
Chance to escape
Exposing my
Inward state
The voice inside
My head says
One foot in front
Of the other
Keep moving
Do not stop
Get in your car

Take a drive

Feel the sunshine

On your face

Today is a

New day

You

Are

Not

Alone

RELEASE

Holding on

Too tight

To things

I cannot

Control

Tension

Held first in

Clenched fists

Raised shoulders

A stiff neck

Its journey

Does not

End there

It travels on

To the heart

Then shows

On my face

The struggle

Within me

Seeping out-

Perhaps the

Solution resides

Within, as well

A cleansing

Breath...in...out

Allowing

Every fiber

To release

The hands

To relax

A full circle

Ending with

Letting go

ROOTS

I keep saying
I'm fine
But I'm not-
Not really
What am I, then?
Sad and afraid
Angry and confused
Wrapped up in one bundle
The flow of opinions
Remains constant-
Whether to feel empowered?
Whether to overpower?
I don't understand-
Absent from
Truth and love
Both are meaningless
And yet, continually,
Thrown like stones
Aimed at an
Invisible target
Except-the target
Is not invisible
It is flesh and blood,
Feelings and emotions

And each stone
Adds another rip
Another cut to
The already worn
So no, *I'm not fine*
But I am learning
When to keep
My opinions
To myself
I am learning
What's important
Roots of truth and love
Holding me steady

THREE SISTERS

Strength, Faith & Fear
It would seem one of
These do not belong
Yet, each share
A space in my thoughts
All together
Arm in arm
Like three inseparable sisters
Each recognizing the role
Of the other two
No one trying to outdo the other
Order of operations, I guess
Fear, being the oldest, relies on prayer-
Opening the door for Faith
The perfect middle sister
What about the youngest?
Her name is Strength!
Her presence eases Fear-
Her presence increases Faith-
Providing assurance that
They belong together
No matter what anyone else says

WEIGHT OF TRUST

Tension grows
Tossing, turning
Desperately
Needing rest
And though
Not out loud-
Crying on
The inside

Like a baby
With heavy eyes
Unable to give
Up the fight
Unable to accept
The balance of
Floating between
Strength and calm

If only the
Little one
Understood-
Giving in for
A few brief
Moments will
Bring perfect,
Peaceful sleep

If only the
Little one
Would trust
Settle into
The strong arms
Simply holding
Tight enough
To offer security

If only
I could
Embrace
The heaviness-
Welcome sleep
And rest
In the calming
Weight of trust

LASTING IMPRESSION

First impressions

Mysteries

Unfinished pictures

Incomplete

Look closer

Each individual

A series of chapters

A personal story

Brushstrokes

In a painting

Notes in a song-

Viewed separately,

Misunderstood-

Experienced together,

A masterpiece-

Understanding

Requires willingness

To trust

To be trusted

Shines light

On the fragments

Solves the puzzle

Reveals the person-

Truly knowing takes time

Oh, what joy
To understand
To experience
This beautiful mystery-
The soul who leaves
A lasting impression

IRREPLACEABLE

Communication advances
Too numerous to count
Words typed in
An email, a text
Instantly sent flying
Across the sky
Reaching its destination
In a matter of seconds
Astonishing advances
And yet, still lacking,
Unable to replace
One unique power
That evokes laughter
Leads to tears and
Instant smiles with
Remember-when's-
And brings instant,
Unimaginable grief
When eternally gone
No longer heard-
Such a sweet sound
The irreplaceable
Voice of a friend

VASTNESS

The vastness
Of this world
Lies beyond my
Understanding-
Both above and
Below the waters
Lives a state of
Continuous motion
Where all move
From life into
Death and
Joy must exist
Alongside grief-
Many are left
In need of rescue-
What happens to
Those searching
Staggering
Feeling only sorrow
Will they fall into
A pit of despair
Or will joyful
Hearts reach out
Their hands into
The vastness
Ready to raise up
Those who grieve
Into the light of
A hopeful embrace

NOISE

So many thoughts
So many voices
Too many words
Constant chatter
Bombarding from
Every direction
Any message of
Importance, hidden
Words needing
To be heard
Seem impossible
To distinguish
From the noise
Stillness required
To hear
My own thoughts
To write
My own words
Carving a path
Through the noise

REFLECTIONS

Yesterday I looked in the mirror
Life out in front
Bright Eyes
Questions
Dreams

Today I looked in the mirror
Half of life behind
Laugh lines
Experiences
Hopes

Tomorrow I will look in the mirror
Where did life go?
Gray hair
Memories
Peace

JOURNEY

Looking back
Thru worried eyes
Ashamed
Dark spots remain
Fear of
Disappointing
The ones
Most loved

Looking back
Thru critical eyes
Dejected
Dark spots grow
Guilt
Weighs down
Body, mind
And soul

Looking back
Thru forgiven eyes
Hopeful
Dark spots fade
In light of
Acceptance
Love
Grace

Looking back
Thru wise eyes
Peaceful
Dark spots transform
Strength
Gained from
Overcoming
While remembering

ONE HUNDRED

I always say
I'd like to live
At least a
Hundred years
Since I'm over
Half-way there
The thought doesn't
Seem so weird
My family will plan
A great big party
Biggest cake
You've ever seen
With one hundred
Sparkling candles
Lighting up
The entire room
Sitting at the piano
I'll play a familiar tune
As party guests loudly sing
Happy birthday to me!
I'll blow out the candles
And make my birthday wish
A hundred-year-old hope
For final peace and rest

LIGHT WAITS

A clear sky
Light of stars
Shining through
The dark night
Gently leads to
Peaceful sleep
Hopeful dreams
For a new day

A cloudy sky
Light of the
Morning star
Covered in gray
Casting doubt
Over the dreams
Of hope from
The night before

A renewed heart
The light of stars
Now hidden-
A radiant memory
Reminding me
That even in the
Darkest of times-
Light waits